Supermodernism

Hans Ibe

Superm

Architect

the Age o

Globaliza

NAi Publ

ngs
dernism
ure in
f
ion

shers

We could

supermoc

that it is

of a coin

obverse r

postmode

positive c

Marc Augé

negative.

say of
ernity
he face
whose
epresents
rnity: the
f a

Non-places: Introduction to an Anthropology of Supermodernity
(London/New York, 1995)

6

Contents

7

Introduct

on

Every age has its own themes, symbols and metaphors. Just as in the 1950s the atom, nuclear energy and the atom bomb occupied a dominant place in popular culture and intellectual debate, so today globalization plays an important role in public opinion. A lot of fashionable nonsense is talked about this subject, but also a good deal of sense. Globalization is so abstract and ephemeral that it can be made to cover just about anything; by the same token, there are so many positive and negative phenomena that can be associated with it, that everyone's daily life at least *seems* to be influenced by it.

Since the early 1990s there have been increasingly frequent pronouncements that much, if not everything that happens nowadays, is either the cause or effect of galloping globalization, from CNN's live coverage of the multi-national victory in the Gulf War to the world-wide financial networks operating in a rarefied cyberspace, from increasing homogenization to inter-cultural creolization.

It is precisely because so many phenomena are associated with globalization that its capacity to explain specific conditions is so limited. In this respect, globalization is rather like the greenhouse effect which laymen and diverse experts hold responsible for both hot and cold summers and for severe as well as mild winters. Nonetheless, the multiplicity of aspects that can be linked to it, only serve to highlight the fact that there are good reasons for regarding globalization as the dominant theme of the 1990s, exerting all kinds of direct and indirect influences on contemporary mentality. The consequences of this are no less noticeable in architecture. On the one hand, the process of internationalization that architecture has undergone since the 1980s can be seen as part of a more general process of globalization. A good many architects have come to regard the world as their oyster. And on the other hand, more and more architects, especially in the affluent part of the world, are beginning to experience globalization - in its many real or perceived forms - as a phenomenon that cannot be ignored, that they must take account of. The growing number of special issues of architectural journals devoted to the causes and effects of globalization and related changes to the built environment is in itself an indication that globalization has become a hot topic equalled only, perhaps, by ecology.

This book has been prompted by a perception of a radical change of direction within architecture during the 1990s, together with the feeling that the new course can be related to the real and putative processes of globalization. After postmodernism and its deconstructivist off-shoot, a new architecture now seems to be emerging, an architecture for which such postmodernist notions as place, context and identity have largely lost their meaning. In the work of architects like Jean Nouvel, Dominique Perrault, OMA, Toyo Ito and dozens of others one begins to discern the contours of an architecture that can no longer be adequately described using the postmodern conceptual framework. To refer to this architecture, a new 'ism' is introduced here: supermodernism. The term is borrowed from the anthropologist Marc Augé who described the supermodern condition in his book *Non-places: Introduction to an Anthropology of Supermodernity* (a translation of *Non-lieux; introduction à une anthropologie de la surmodernité*, Paris 1992), claiming that it manifests itself chiefly in the way people deal with place and space nowadays.

This book is neither a critique of nor an ode to globalization or the architecture that may be a consequence of it. Just as a meteorologist charts the weather without directly passing judgement on the greenhouse theory, so this book discusses recent phenomena inside and outside architecture in the knowledge that these phenomena are - rightly or wrongly - seen in relation to globalization processes.

11

Postmode

rnism

In recent decades, architecture and architectural discourse has been dominated by postmodernism. As a style, postmodernism has always been contentious but as a school of thought, its ideas have been pretty well universally accepted. Even staunch opponents of a postmodernist style hold opinions that reflect a postmodern mentality. The essence of this mentality is a rejection not only of modern architecture but also of such modern concepts as a belief in progress and faith in reason. During the past twenty years, this mentality has played a crucial role in architectural culture in much of the northern hemisphere and in the affluent regions of the southern hemisphere.

13

Modern architecture was rejected because, seen from a postmodernist perspective, it had degenerated since 1945 into an anonymous product for the biggest common denominator: visually impoverished, technocratic, large-scale and indifferent to people and context alike.

The alternatives devised since the 1950s to overcome these shortcomings of modern architecture are exceedingly diverse and range all the way from Aldo van Eyck's humane structuralism to Robert Stern's historicizing eclecticism. This in itself indicates that architecture after modernism cannot easily be lumped together under one heading. Huge diversity is also a feature of the book that gave postmodernism a historiographical identity, Charles Jencks's *The Language of Post-Modern Architecture* (London, 1977), which appeared two years before François Lyotard's *La condition postmoderne* (Paris, 1979), the standard work of postmodern philosophy. Jencks's book marked the breakthrough of postmodernism as a concept in the architectural world. The revisions and additions of later editions served to present postmodernism more strongly as a specific style: a mostly classically-inspired historicizing style, richly embellished with figurative and therefore easily understood symbolic ornaments.

Jencks's idiosyncratic book, which is both a witty analysis of the new architectural approach taking shape in the 1970s, and a scathing criticism of the deficiencies of modern architecture, is not necessarily the most representative reflection of postmodernist ideas. But it does contain two key reproaches levelled by postmodernists at modernists: a dearth of communicative skills and a lack of memory. The main assumption underlying Jencks's book is that architecture can be construed as - to borrow a term from those days - a linguistic system. Influenced by the growing popularity of semiotics, the idea arose that everything, from fashion to visual art, could be interpreted as wordless language. Jencks's criticism of modern architecture focused on modern architects' inability to speak this wordless language and to convey meanings related to the purpose of the building in question. In order to prove his point, Jencks compared the outward appearance of two buildings, the boiler house and the chapel, designed by Mies van de Rohe for the Illinois Institute of Technology in Chicago. After claiming that he was unable to discern any appreciable differences between the two buildings, Jencks feigned confusion as to whether this should be interpreted as a devaluation of religion or a revaluation of central heating.

Jencks was not the only one to blame modern architecture's abstraction for its apparent inability to propagate symbolic messages. During the 1970s and 80s it was customary to describe modern architecture as expressionless and dull because it lacked complexity and contradiction, to paraphrase the title of a celebrated book by Robert Venturi published in 1966.

The insights of semiotics, it must be said, have made little lasting contribution to architectural criticism and history. What has remained, however, is the idea that every building is, in semiotic jargon, a 'bearer of meaning', a conception that led to special attention being paid to the symbolic dimension of architecture. Over the last twenty years, the notion that architecture can to a large extent be understood as a communicative system has become an *idée reçue*. Just what a building can communicate, apart from the fact that it exists, is an open question for which there are

ldo Rossi, Cemitary San Cataldo, Modena, Italy, 1972

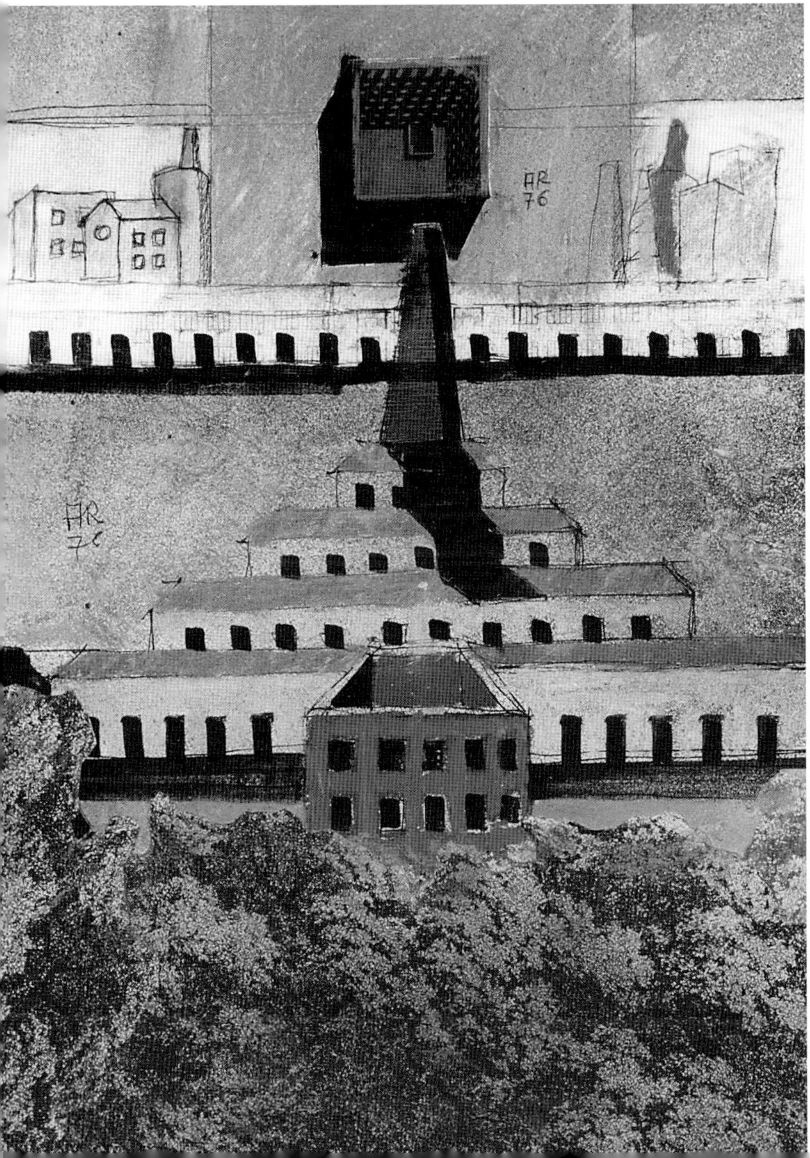

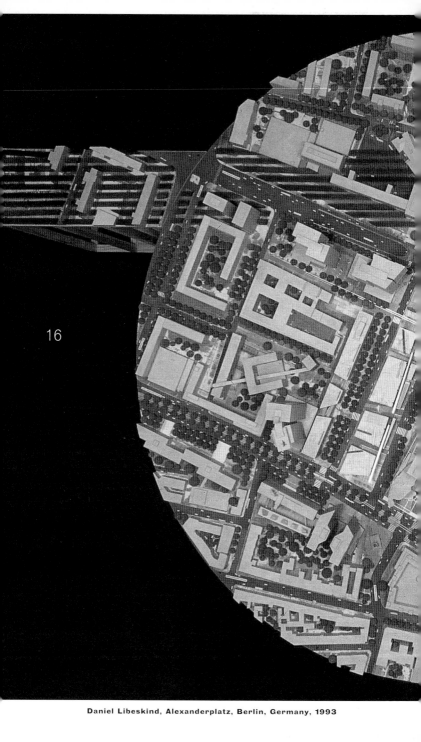

16

Daniel Libeskind, Alexanderplatz, Berlin, Germany, 1993

dozens of possible answers. In an age of 'anything goes', what it came down to was that every building was supposed, one way or another, to contain references - another typical 1980s word - to something or other. Usually they were references to architecture, architectural history, the context or whatever went on inside the building, but increasingly buildings started to function as vehicles for ideas that had nothing at all to do with architecture. In the heyday of post-modernism, allusion was a party game for architects and their critics who busied themselves respectively with the deployment and decipherment of allusions. Allusion - especially to context - was also one of the most frequently used means of legitimizing architecture. If there was one point that was emphasized in postmodernism, it was that a building must fit in with its surroundings and - to quote the phrase that Tom Wolfe ridiculed in *From Bauhaus to Our House* (New York, 1981) - enter into a dialogue with it. Modern architecture, it was generally opined, had nothing to say and thus remained silent.

From the postmodernist perspective, sensitivity to context and the assimilation of elements from its surroundings are what give a building its right to exist. The lip-service architects are so fond of paying to contextualism is perhaps an even clearer example of this than contextualist architecture itself, which in many cases is only partially successful in inserting itself into the context. The contextualist position is chiefly informed by the concept of *genius loci*, the subject of an influential book of that name by Christian Norberg-Schulz, which is based on the idea that each site has its own specific character that is dictated by location, geography and history. One of the aims of architecture was to reveal the spirit of the site by laying bare hidden traces of place and history. Sometimes this assumed bizarre forms, as in the work of Peter Eisenman who has applied himself, in 'artificial excavations', to exposing invisible and non-existent traces, a passion he shares with Daniel Libeskind. The latter's free associations with location and context are like an intellectual delirium in which everything seems to be related to everything else, and they give rise to an unintended parody on the pseudo-profundity that has afflicted architecture since the rise of postmodernism. Actually, alongside the elitist allusions barely comprehensible to the uninitiated, postmodernism has always had a populist tendency committed to 'giving people what they want': a readily accessible symbolism designed to appeal to everyone.

Behind every form of contextualism, however intellectual or populist, lurks the moralistic idea that somehow or other it is a good thing for new buildings to relate to what already is or has been. The idea that the pre-existing is beautiful and valuable is of less importance here than the conviction that respect for what already exists or has existed, is morally superior to the propensity to demolish everything and to begin with a clean slate. The gay abandon with which buildings were demolished, redeveloped and converted until well into the 1970s, consequently gave way to a high degree of circumspection. In the last instance, the only architecture shown no consideration by postmodernism was post-war modernism which, according to the heir to the British throne and honorary architectural critic, Prince Charles, had caused more damage than German bombing during the Second World War.

One of the arguments in favour of a cautious approach to the built environment was based on the growing perception that many people, for whatever reason, are attached to what is already there and familiar. Some even went so far as to claim that the built environment is an essential point of reference in daily life. That buildings, spaces, neighbourhoods, cities, monuments function as prompts, not only for individuals but also for whole communities. This position was articulated by Aldo Rossi in 1966 in *L'architettura della città*, a book that in the 1980s (after it had appeared in other languages) retrospectively came to be regarded as one of the theoretical foundations of postmodernism. Rossi had assigned the built environment the role of personal and collective *aide mémoire* in the context of his concept of the analogue city that exists in everybody's imagination: a highly personal version of the city consisting of buildings, streets, squares and parks associated with particular memories.

Venturi, Scott Brown and Associates, Gordon Wu Hall, Butler College, Princeton University, Princeton, USA, 1983

Parallel with the discovery of memory as a medium for channelling meaning in architecture, was the discovery of architecture's own memory. One aspect of postmodernism is its (re)discovery of history as a value-free source of inspiration and as an inexhaustible repertoire of forms, types, styles, and so on, that everyone is free to re-cycle at their own discretion. Simply put, the modernists regarded the

21

Leon Krier, reconstruction of Place du Nouveau Parlement and conversion of existing administration tower, Luxemburg, 1973-1978

past - with the exception of the particular line in history from which they claimed descent - as just so much dead weight. For postmodernists the past was the natural starting-point for the creation of something new. What is more, they discovered an infectious delight in the past, for it turned out that there was so much more to discover there than the Palladio-Ledoux-Schinkel line of descent. One of the most lasting salutary effects of postmodernism is that a good deal of previously neglected architectural history is now the subject of research. This in turn has resulted in a more

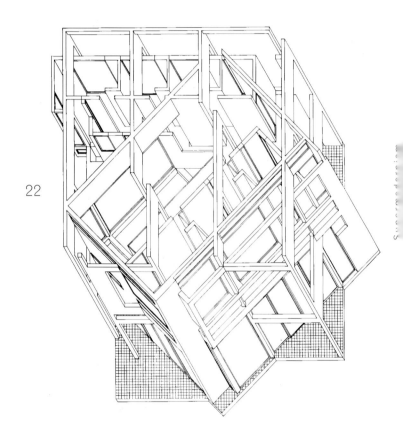

Supermodernism

Peter Eisenman, House III, Lakeville (Connecticut), USA, 1969-1971

nuanced view of history than is to be found in such out-and-out modernist books as Sigfried Giedion's *Space, Time and Architecture* (Cambridge Mass., 1941).

During the past twenty years, the history of their own discipline has been the main source of reference for postmodernist architects. But they have also eagerly embraced all manner of non-architectural allusions, from the readily accessible figurative symbolism favoured by American postmodernists and borrowed from Las Vegas, road-side architecture, Disney cartoons and what have you, to more recondite allusions to recent philosophical and scientific insights. The founding father of labyrinthine allusions is Peter Eisenman. Since the late 1960s Eisenman has been at pains to give concrete expression to Noam Chomsky's language theory in designs and buildings. While the attempts themselves have received extensive coverage in recent architectural historiography, their usefulness has never been subjected to serious consideration. Eisenman has been followed by a flood of architects claiming to find legitimation for their designs outside architecture in areas about which they probably understand less than they do about architecture. For many architects, the insights of philosophy formed the main justification for their actions. They adopted an analogous style of argumentation whereby what holds for philosophy also holds for architecture, an idea that was no doubt prompted by the fact that both disciplines had a postmodernist 'school'. Although they did not have all that much in common, homonymity was evidently sufficient grounds for assuming a certain affinity.

Central to postmodern philosophy were its many and varied attempts to dismantle the modernist mind-set, in which short work was made of such modernist certainties as progress, objectivity and originality. The point of departure for such endeavours was the conviction that the 'grand discourses' or 'grand narratives', such as those spun by the Enlightenment and Modernism, had run their course, lost their validity or been rendered obsolete by time or the course of events. Belief in progress and meta-discourses made way for relativism and equivalence. On the face of it, philosophers were concerned with the same themes as architects - after all, modernist notions were put into perspective in postmodernist architecture too - and as such it seemed only natural to make a connection between architecture and philosophy. It seemed even more logical when philosophers and architects started to work together, as in the case of Eisenman and Jacques Derrida, in order, through dialogue, to arrive at architectural designs with a high philosophical content. Architects without access to their own personal philosopher had to make do with books. For countless architects in Europe and on the East Coast of America, essays by predominantly French thinkers like Derrida, Jean Baudrillard, Gilles Deleuze and François Lyotard became as much a part of their routine reading matter as architectural journals. In terms of individual intellectual enrichment, these philosophical studies may have been very rewarding; architecture itself, however, gained little from the exercise. The problem was that designers got no further than a usually fairly literal architectural interpretation of mental constructs, a practice that reached its high point in deconstructivism. Here Derrida's philosophy of deconstruction was converted into a pseudo-chaos of oblique angles, and Deleuze's metaphor of the fold was translated into folded floors and walls.

Around 1990, deconstructivism was presented as a break with postmodernism, but beneath the outward differences the two movements had a good many things in common. Deep down, deconstructivism is no more than a mannerist reversal of the postmodernist notions of place, identity and meaning, a reversal which, though it puts them in a different perspective, nonetheless recognizes them as fundamental. Moreover, like postmodernism, deconstructivism rests on the pillar of symbolic meaning whereby architectural form is seen as metaphorical. Strictly speaking, the only real difference between the two 'isms' is that in recent years postmodernism has attained a strong position as an acceptable, universally applicable style, whereas the only foothold deconstructivist architecture has managed to secure in the architectural arena has been within the conditioned setting of exhibitions, publications in books and journals and the odd commission, chiefly in the cultural domain.

The mannerist side of deconstructivism is apparent not only in the ostensible *Umwertung aller Werte* and the undermining of all certainties, but also in the movement's recent super-refinement in the direction of complex geometry which, according to insiders like Peter Davidson and Donald L. Bates (*Architectural Design Profile* 127), should be termed 'after geometry'. Here architecture is transformed into a geometrical game of skill for architects, just as the mannerism which followed the Renaissance was a game played with the devices of classical architecture. One thing is certain, in deconstructivism issues like social relevance, functionality and all sorts of pragmatic aspects are consciously or unconsciously brushed aside as tedious demands that hamper the free expression of the individual. For deconstructivism, far more than postmodernism which still had a populist side capable of appealing to the man in the street, is a movement for connoisseurs. This coterie is regarded as authoritative in an artificial situation in which a presence in various printed and digital media, at exhibitions and congresses, is considered more important than making a concrete contribution to architecture, let alone offering a solution for the countless practical problems facing designers. It is in precisely this kind of universe that architects like Eisenman, Libeskind, Bernard Tschumi and Lebbeus Woods have been able to acquire the status of pop stars whose every new utterance is awaited with bated breath.

Unlike in the 1960s, when architects functioned primarily as rational problem-solvers and applied their creativity to practical issues, the work of architects in the age of postmodernism has more than ever acquired an autobiographical dimension. As a consequence, it seems as if all sorts of personal obsessions, hobbies and opinions have become more relevant for their work than the brief and the programme. Architecture has become a form of artistic self-expression in which designs and buildings are reflections of personal associations and personal world-views, in the same way as visual art has, since the Romantic era, been interpreted as a personal expression of the artistic individual. This personalization of architecture is not the only similarity with pop stardom. The comparison goes even further: nowadays star architects are continually 'on tour': for competitions, juries, teaching posts, master-classes, interviews, conferences and lectures, interspersed with the odd construction meeting. Just like pop stars, these star architects have all developed a clear and considered media strategy. They have also become increasingly preoccupied with merchandising. In the days when these stars had scarcely a realized building to their name, their most marketable products were their designs (which earned them the pejorative title of 'paper architect'), but these were soon joined by all manner of household goods - dinner services, cutlery, serving trays, coffee pots, whistling kettles, small items of furniture and so on. Such affordable products sparked off a collecting drive among all those anxious to surround themselves with 'good' design, a hobby for a well-to-do elite of trendsetters and followers. The same collecting fervour then began to manifest itself in relation to architecture. Numerous cities in the capitalist world appear to have been engaged in a game of happy families over the past fifteen years, for they all seem to possess at least one building by each of the big-name architects. This has happened on a grand scale in Berlin where in the 1980s the Internationale Bauausstellung (IBA) gave the most heterogeneous collection of architects an opportunity to build and in the 1990s the fall of the Wall triggered off a new string of commissions for an elite line-up of international master builders. The same phenomenon occurs on a smaller scale. Even a relatively small city like The Hague has been enriched with work by *inter alia* Alvaro Siza, Ricardo Bofill, Richard Meier, Rob Krier, Michael Graves, Cesar Pelli and Henri Ciriani.

 This previously unknown passion for collecting architecture is related to the main reasons for postmodernism's international success: the

Mario Botta, private house, Stabio, Switzerland, 1980-1982

immediately identifiable personal signature of the protagonists, regardless of *where* they build. This applies to Mario Botta in southern Switzerland or France, Frank Gehry in France or Spain, Richard Meier in Spain or the US, Arata Isozaki in the US or Japan and to Aldo Rossi in Japan or Italy. The global distribution of the work of these and many other architects underlines the extent to which the personal signature has become a unique selling point in architecture. As a result, one of the original hallmarks

Mario Botta, San Francisco Museum of Modern Art, San Francisco, USA, 1989-1995

of postmodernism, sensitivity to place, context and regional idiosyncrasies, has been pushed into the background. Its merit was discovered in reaction to the alleged international uniformity of modern architecture and in a way this quality has made architects like Botta and Rossi famous. In the light of its original ideals, the fact that postmodernism can in the final analysis be compared with the much-criticized *International Style*, could perhaps be seen as retrograde. But in many respects it is a logical consequence of the trend towards internationalization set in motion in the 1980s.

Frank O. Gehry & Associates, Nationale Nederlanden Office Building,
Prague, Czech Republic, 1991-1996

Aldo Rossi, Hotel Il Palazzo, Fukuoka, Japan, 1987

Moderr

ism

Modernism, and certainly the post-war version of it, has come in for some pretty harsh criticism over the last two decades. But after years of debunking everything that smacked of modernity there are signs that the tide is turning. The architecture of the immediate post-war years is gradually winning more appreciation, in part for the very same reasons that earned it so much criticism in the 1970s and 80s. In this age of globalization, the ideas underlying the *International Style* - that an architectural style or approach should be internationally applicable - have acquired new significance. It was this international quality that postmodernists had vehemently objected to from the very beginning.

Worldwide success, however, has turned postmodernism into just such a universally applied style as the modernism to which it was a reaction. The main difference is that whereas the international quality of postmodernism is the paradoxical by-product of a movement that turned its back on international architecture, modernism was consciously international. The worldwide dissemination of *International Style* modernism in the 1950s and 60s coincided with the deliberate cultivation of the quality of 'internationality' which was seen as an essential element of modernity. In those days, internationality still possessed the aura of glamour associated with the lifestyle of the happy few, the aptly named 'jet set'. The expression 'jet set' is almost forgotten nowadays when millions of tourists think nothing of a flight in a jet airliner and worldwide telephone, fax and data communications are everyday phenomena. National borders and time zones are, mentally at least, no longer a barrier to any kind of interchange. In this respect, the 1990s can be seen as the superlative of the modernist 1950s and 60s which in turn represented an amplification of prewar processes of modernization and internationalization. In the modern movement there has always been a strong connection between being up to date and being international. Functionalism was described as an international architecture in the 1920s (Walter Gropius, *Internationale Architektur* (Munich, 1925)) and in the 1930s the book published in connection with the *Modern Architecture* exhibition at the New York Museum of Modern Art, *The International Style: Architecture Since 1922* (New York, 1932), put the seal on the international character of modern architecture. Almost simultaneously, Alberto Sartoris's *Gli elementi dell'architettura funzionale* (Milan, 1932) demonstrated just how international this *International Style* had become. Hundreds of examples from a wide variety of countries proved beyond doubt that modern architecture had given rise to an international mode of building.

In the 1950s and 60s, there was an even stronger sense that things were the same all the world over. The ubiquitous modern architecture was both the clearest proof of this and a major contributing factor, witness Udo Kultermann's *New Architecture in the World* (New York, 1965), a book that impresses not so much by its text as by its subtle, associative collection of pictures of buildings from the unlikeliest corners of the world which together give the impression of a coherent world architecture. The suggestion that one mode of building had started to predominate throughout the world was reinforced by the fact that modern architects had taken to building beyond their own national borders. In the 1950s, led by American and naturalized American architects like Mies van der Rohe, Walter Gropius, Marcel Breuer and Skidmore, Owings & Merrill, there developed for the first time an international architectural practice. As an affluent world power, the United States was a natural touchstone for this international architecture, one example being the big hotel where modernity and internationalism coincided. In the 1950s and 60s modern hotels shot up all over the world, from Helsinki to Miami Beach and from London to Tokyo, hotels which may have belonged to different companies but which nevertheless could be seen as part of one big - American - chain. As such they were the first true exemplars of world architecture. This congruity was not merely the result of the rapid emergence of a

Skidmore, Owings & Merill, Inland Steel Company Headquarters Building, Chicago, USA, 1956-1958

convention on what a luxury hotel should look like. Equally important was the fact that this uniformity, relieved at most by the occasional touch of local colour, provided international businessmen and wealthy globetrotters with a familiar refuge from the dynamic world outside.

The hotel was not the only building type for which modernism had a standard model in stock. The same is true of a host of other genres, such as the office building which has been deployed around the world in the shape of the 'glass box'.

Viljo Rewell and Keyo Petäjä, Palace Hotel, Helsinki, Finland, 1952

The presence of such virtually identical buildings on every continent suggested not only that the differences in the speed of development of countries in the First, Second and Third Worlds were decreasing and that prosperity was just around the corner for everybody, but also that events were taking place more or less simultaneously all over the world. In the 1950s and 60s, more than at any time in the past, there was a conviction that people everywhere belonged to one and the same global community. Thanks to tele-communications and improvements in intercontinental

H.A. Maaskant, Hilton Hotel, Rotterdam, the Netherlands, 1964

Arne Jacobsen, SAS Royal Hotel and Air Terminal, Copenhagen, Denmark, 1959

connections, so the argument went, it had become relatively easy to take an active part in this global society. Such sentiments are today once again being expressed on all sides. Nowadays the contention that we all live in one world is supported by pointing to the fact that in today's global society the same products can be bought everywhere and the same television stations can be received everywhere.

Back then, the idea of the emergence of a global community was based on the idealistic hope that after the Second World War a new era of lasting peace had dawned. Today the idealistic component consists in the hope that thanks to worldwide communication networks, no one need any longer be deprived of any information in the 'global village' that is now closer at hand than ever before.

Far-reaching external similarities in post-war modern architecture are not confined to such mundane building types as offices and housing blocks, where standardization can be explained in terms of economics. Oddly enough, uniformity also manifests itself in singular structures like conference halls, theatres, exhibition complexes, churches and stadiums. However seemingly original their appearance, there is usually a building somewhere that looks like them, is based on the same principles or employs a similar construction system. The last is particularly common. In the 1950s and 60s architects tended to view a commission to design one of these 'unique' structures as an invitation to pull out all the stops on new materials and new construction methods. The result was gargantuan spans, extravagant projections and intricately formed, ultra-thin shell roofs by architects and engineers like Pierluigi Nervi, Matthew Nowicki, Kenzo Tange, Eero Saarinen, Jorn Utzon and Hugh Stubbins. Their works demonstrate the possibilities of contemporary technology and, in the unfortunate case of Stubbins's Berlin conference hall which collapsed 23 years after completion in 1980, unintentionally the impossibilities, too. What characterizes all these bold structures is an overt display of daring ingenuity. Each of these unique buildings has entailed sifting through a bottomless bag of technological tricks for just those devices

Kenzo Tange, Olympic stadium, Tokyo, Japan, 1960-1964

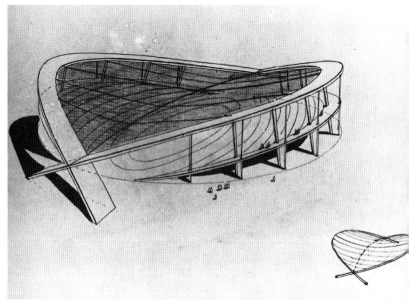

Matthew Nowicki, Dorton Arena (preliminary design), Raleigh, USA, 1948

capable of delivering an effect that is, quite literally, sensational. The immediate sensation of space, form and light, of transparency and weightlessness is more important in this modern architecture than the communication of any message.

Around 1970, the use of sophisticated technology shifted from the construction to the services which have much less impact on the appearance of a building. This love affair with services engineering culminated in the 1970s in one of the most important gadgets of the day, the control panel. With this built-in forerunner of the remote control unit it was possible - in a private home for instance - to regulate temperature, light, ventilation, sun blinds, quadrophonic music, television screens, sliding walls and rotating and height-adjustable plateaus, to name the functions of just a few of the most important buttons.

The fascination with services engineering during the 1970s served to keep alive a modern tradition of technological innovation that was to blossom at end of the decade into the high tech movement. In high tech the interest in both structural and services engineering coincided in an architecture that strove to keep pace with technological developments taking place outside architecture, for example in aviation, space travel and the automobile industry. During the postmodern years this approach was an awkward feature of the architectural panorama. In most cases such architecture was judged not on its innovative technology but on a merit it scarcely possessed: the symbolic dimension. Rather than being seen for what it was - new technology - high tech was seen as an allusion to cars and aeroplanes, to science fiction if need be. Yet high tech is only incidentally symbolic, just as the ocean steamer motifs in Le Corbusier's work are of only minor importance.

Another modern tendency kept alive by high tech is what from a postmodern perspective could be regarded as a lack of interest in any form of adjustment to the surroundings. It was in these terms for example that Diane Ghirardo recently criticized Norman Foster's Century Tower in Tokyo in *Architecture After Modernism* (London, 1995): 'Whatever its merits, this ... building could quite

Staffan Berglund, villa Spies, Torö, Sweden, 1967-1969

literally have been built anywhere, even though the design was conditioned by local site constraints.' The autonomous relationship with the city and the landscape that Ghirardo detects in Foster's work can be seen as an essential feature of modernism. Modern architects rejected mimicry, indeed they consciously sought to make their work stand out from its surroundings. They achieved the desired contrast by using elementary geometric forms, employing new materials and methods of construction and by taking no account of the size of the surrounding buildings. The result was that modern architects steadfastly did the same thing, whether the building site was on Wall Street in downtown New York, near Wren's St. Paul's Cathedral in the centre of London or in the middle of a virgin landscape in Africa. Probably the most important motive behind this independence from specific conditions, was the idea that modern architecture was by definition a new beginning and a break with the past. This explains why modern architects were so attracted to the concept of the tabula rasa defined only by length and breadth. The idea that the site can be seen as an immaculate, empty expanse may have been branded reprehensible by the postmodernists, but from a modernist point of view it is eminently sensible. Modern architects have always regarded it as more important that their work should be in keeping with the age than in harmony with the surroundings.

The maximum concession modern architects were prepared to make to the surroundings was a certain neutrality, although in most cases this led to an ostentatious unobtrusiveness. During the postmodern period, this minimalist neutrality was severely criticized for its alleged meaninglessness but this ignored a unique quality of such architecture: its ability, through total abstraction, to evoke a deafening silence. Seen in this light, the modern architecture of Mies van der Rohe, for example, is blessed with tremendous expressive power, comparable to the paintings of such abstract expressionists as Barnett Newman which impress precisely because of their limited resources.

Given that this aesthetic of 'less is more' has

Ludwig Mies van der Rohe, masterplan for the Illinois Institute of Technology, Chicago,

USA, 1940

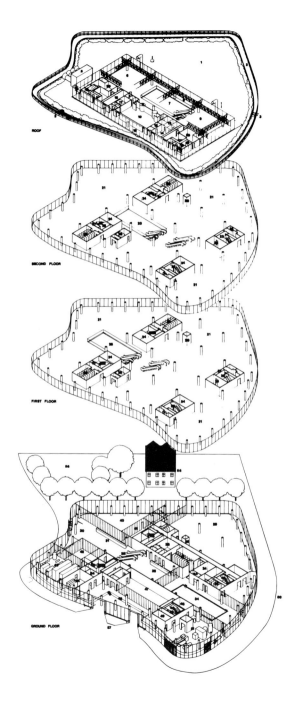

Norman Foster, Willis, Faber & Dumas Head Office, Ipswich, Great Britain, 1970-1975

Norman Foster, Century Tower, Tokyo, Japan, 1991

John Pawson, Wakaba restaurant, London, Great Britain, 1987

enjoyed an considerable revival in recent years, post-war modernism can be seen as relevant to current practice. A closer analysis of the much-maligned International Style is certainly in order. Today's minimalism, incidentally, is purer than ever before, thanks to improvements in technology and materials. This purity is found both in the extraordinarily aesthetic architecture of the likes of Tadao Ando, Wiel Arets and John Pawson, and in the 'almost nothing' of today's average glass box, the shape of which is also more abstract than ever before. This abstraction stands in stark contrast to the postmodernist extravagance and deconstructivist complexity that have constituted the aesthetic frame of reference for the past two decades. This simplicity is not primarily a reaction to the aesthetic of visual excess, although that aspect certainly plays a role. In essence, the new abstraction is an expression of a fundamentally different attitude to architecture which it sees less and less as significant and filled with symbolic meaning, and more and more as a neutral object.

H.A. Maaskant, Tomado office building, Dordrecht, the Netherlands, 1958-1962

Supermod

ernism

In 1990 an exhibition at the Museum of Modern Art in New York launched deconstructivism as the latest architectural movement. Ever since the *Modern Architecture* exhibition held in that same museum in 1932, every MoMA exhibition devoted to a new group or movement has been regarded as an important signal, as confirmation of the movement's significance and as official recognition. The fact that Philip Johnson, almost sixty years after his first success exhibition, was involved behind the scenes of the deconstructivism exhibition served to reinforce the idea that there really was something going on here. Seen in retrospect, deconstructivism was destined to be short-lived. The rot set in at an early stage when various architects included in the exhibition declared that they wanted no part of it. Even the reverberations set off by the exhibition were quick to die down. Initially, deconstructivism received a lot of attention in journals like *Architectural Design* which for a few years filled its columns with deconstructivist designs and deconstructivist interpretations, but nowadays architecture that might still perhaps be called deconstructivist is a scarce commodity and the word is seldom used any more. The guru of deconstruction, the French philosopher Jacques Derrida, is likewise having to contend with dwindling popularity, as was painfully obvious during the *Anyhow* conference in Rotterdam (1997) where there seemed to be a tacit embargo on Derrida's name.

The expectation that MoMA's *Deconstructivist Architecture* exhibition would change the course of architectural history has come to nothing and that has probably helped to ensure that people will henceforth be less inclined to attach special significance to an architectural exhibition in the MoMA. Perhaps this partly explains why a recent interesting but less heavily hyped MoMA exhibition, Terence Riley's *Light Construction* (1995), has received relatively little attention. Although the foreword to the accompanying

Phillipe Starck, Baron Vert Building, Osaka, Japan, 1990-1992

publication makes a cautious attempt to let some of the shine of *Modern Architecture* rub off on *Light Architecture*, the exhibition has not been all that well received. Interestingly, the idea behind this exhibition is a good deal more provocative than the 1990 attempt to grant deconstructivism a status that it had already enjoyed for quite some time.

Light Construction (1995) is all about the lightness of contemporary architecture. Glassy, transparent and translucent buildings are suddenly popping up all over the place, from Japan and the United States to Spain and Switzerland. At least as characteristic as their ephemeral appearance is the fact that these structures are rarely if ever the product of formal considerations: 'In telling contrast to the ultimate importance given to architectural form in both historicist postmodernism and deconstructivism, many of these projects exhibit a remarkable lack of concern for, if not antipathy toward, formal considerations. In fact, most of the projects could be described by a phrase no more complicated than "rectangular volume".' Riley sees the subordination of formal concerns as part and parcel of the 'new architectural sensibility' that *Light Construction* was intended to trace. Nor is he the only one to have observed such changes. A book published in Italy earlier the same year, *Architettura in superficie; materiali, figure e tecnologie delle nuove facciate urbane* (Rome, 1995) by Daniela Colafranceschi, was devoted to the rise of the smooth, transparent or translucent facade.

Almost simultaneously another book appeared: *Monolithic Architecture* (Munich/New York, 1995) by Rodolfo Machado and Rodolphe el-Khoury. It described the trend towards buildings that look as if they have been made in one piece, buildings with the capacity 'to deliver tremendous eloquence with very limited formal means'. In most cases these are solid, massive structures, but occasionally they are light, transparent constructions some of which are also included in Riley's selection.

A year later, Vittorio Savi and Josep Mª Montaner published *Less is More: Minimalism in Architecture and the Other Arts* (Barcelona, 1996), another book that had much in common with Riley's exhibition. *Less*

Toyo Ito, ITM Building, Matsuyama, Japan, 1993

Peter Zumthor, Kunsthaus Bregenz, Bregenz, Austria, 1991-1996

Kazuyo Sejima & Associates, Gifu Kitagata Housing, Motosu, Japan, 1994-1999

Kazuyo Sejima & Associates, Saishunkan Seiyaku Women's Dormitory, Kumamoto, Japan, 1991

is More deals with the aesthetic minimalism that has been gaining prominence since the beginning of the 1990s and places it in the context of the visual arts and the history of architecture. Here, too, the focus is on an abstract architecture that refers to nothing outside itself and here, too, a lot of attention is devoted to formal reduction.

In all four publications, the same or at least similar themes are dealt with and the same architectural offices crop up (often represented by the selfsame structures): Jean Nouvel, Dominique Perrault, Philippe Starck, Rem Koolhaas's OMA, Toyo Ito and Herzog & De Meuron. The striking similarities suggest that all four books are busy elucidating different aspects of one and the same architectural phenomenon, of one and the same sensibility, which could perhaps be designated 'supermodernism'.

This sensibility manifests itself not only in Riley's lightness and transparency, Colafranceschi's smooth facade, Machado and El-Khoury's monolith or Savi and Montaner's minimalism. In more general terms, it can be characterized as a sensitivity to the neutral, the undefined, the implicit, qualities that are not confined to architectural substance but also find powerful expression in a new spatial sensibility, an aspect that receives little attention in the four books. The spatial changes are nonetheless crucial to recent architecture. After the explicitly defined spatiality of postmodernism and deconstructivism, it looks as if the - decades-old - ideal of boundless and undefined space is set to become the main *Leitbild* for architects. This boundless space is no dangerous wilderness or frightening emptiness, but rather a controlled vacuum, for if there is one thing that characterizes this age it is total control. The undefined space is not an emptiness but a safe container, a flexible shell.

From a strictly art-historical perspective, the rise of such notions as undefinedness, boundlessness and neutrality can be seen as a reaction to the ruling tendency of the preceding, postmodern, period. Yet it is also possible to look outside architecture for an explanation for changes within the architectural domain. The first thing that to present itself is the complex of phenomena collectively known as

Herzog & De Meuron, Central Signal Box 4, Basel, Switzerland, 1994-1997

'globalization'. Inevitably, increased mobility and telecommunications and the rise of new media, all of which have been ascribed a major role in the globalization process, also affect architecture and urban planning in that they alter our experience of time and - especially relevant in this context - space. Although cause and effect have become inextricably entangled in discussions about globalization, so that it is difficult to say precisely what its effects are, international interrelatedness and the emergence of worldwide networks in an ephemeral cyberspace have undoubtedly changed our perception of the world. As a consequence, the world, especially for the inhabitants of the affluent northern hemisphere, has become both smaller and larger. Smaller, because everything is, if not in reality then certainly electronically, closer; larger, because thanks to telecommunications, the rising tide of information and ever-increasing mobility, a larger portion of the world is one way or another familiar, seems familiar or is assumed to be familiar. It is easy to predict that mobility will continue to increase worldwide as long as prosperity continues to rise. Increasing prosperity is the most important factor in growing mobility, as is evident from the results of a study cited recently in a special transportation issue of *Scientific American* (October 1997). It seems that all over the world, mobility varies in direct proportion to income, irrespective of the means of transport and irrespective of the level of income, at the rate of one kilometre for every dollar of income.

Although the individual's radius of action continues to expand as a result of increasing mobility, space itself is being steadily reduced to a zone that is traversed, an interval in a continuous movement interrupted at most for a brief stopover. Scarcely anybody has a clearly formulated opinion about this transit zone. Most seem indifferent to what this in-between space looks like, accepting it as inevitable, something about which it is pointless or unnecessary to have, say, an aesthetic opinion. Herein lies a paradox of the expanding world, for while the area designated as familiar territory is larger than ever before, people find the world less and less meaningful, precisely because a large portion of the known world is familiar only from a fleeting visit and is not a place, with which people feel some affinity, where they feel at home, where they actually meet other people rather than being simply thrown together by chance.

The meaninglessness of the built environment, or rather the experience of that meaninglessness, is one of the themes of Marc Augé's (*Non-places: Introduction to an Anthropology of Supermodernity* (New York, 1995)). This book hinges on the difference between place (lieu) and space (espace), where place is defined in anthropological terms as an area that has acquired meaning as a result of human activities. Augé's contention is that a growing proportion of space lacks meaning in the classic anthropological sense because nobody feels any attachment to it. He sees this phenomenon as one of the three forms of abundance characterizing what he terms the supermodern condition: an abundance of space, an abundance of signs (in today's society everybody is constantly being bombarded with information) and an 'abundance of individualization'. This third factor, too, is highly relevant to architecture in that radical individualization affects the use of public and semi-public space which is seen less as social space than as an area that everybody uses individually.

Those places to which nobody feels any special attachment and which do not function in a traditional manner as meeting places, Augé dubs 'non-places'. According to him the world is increasingly made up of such non-places which are particularly common in the sphere of mobility and consumption. Airports, hotels, supermarkets, shopping malls, motorway stops and so on are all places where people occasionally spend varying lengths of time, but the function of these spaces is quite different from, say, the village square which is the social centre of a community. The small group of people who do want to use spaces like shopping malls, supermarkets and station halls as traditional public space, consists for the most part of tramps, alcoholics and drug addicts, people in whom such behaviour is definitely not appreciated and who are often not tolerated in worlds that are increasingly controlled by surveillance: less and less by guards and more and more by video systems that, in combination with all manner of magnetic cards and pin codes, seem to make the presence of flesh and blood people redundant. In short, public space has changed from a meeting place, the heart of social life, into a highly regulated domain where every individual imagines him or herself secure and also takes it for granted that this security is guaranteed. The control is not social control but surveillance by a third party who is supposed to ensure the safety of the individual and at the same time relieve that same individual of the obligation to look after his or her own safety.

The non-places Augé writes about, seem to turn up everywhere and everywhere to look the same. All over the world, supermarkets, shopping malls, hotels and airports have adopted a similar, recognizable form, acquiring an element of familiarity in their tacit uniformity. Although Augé does not use the word, these non-places can be seen as typical expressions of the age of globalization.

GLOBALIZATION

The most comprehensive research into the phenomenon of globalization has been carried out by sociologists.* The results are as diverse as the interpretations of the word itself. For a start, one or two even question whether there is any such thing as globalization or whether it is not simply, in the classic Marxist sense of the word, an ideology. In a similar vein is the suggestion that globalization is a phenomenon as old as the hills that has at best acquired a more prominent place in our consciousness these days. Even among those who claim to have recognized a genuinely existing globalization as a typical contemporary phenomenon, there are conflicting opinions as to what its effects might be. Moreover, there is no consensus as to whether globalization is a condition in itself or a consequence, for example of the processes of modernization. And by extension, there is no consensus either about whether globalization should be linked to modernity, postmodernity or even supermodernity. Another substantial difference of opinion, certainly among sociologists, concerns the effects of globalization.

Some see chiefly homogenizing effects while others claim to detect increasing heterogeneity. A third position is taken by those who discern a 'glocalization' whereby the very process of homogenization serves to emphasize the specific, the local and the authentic. A step further, finally, is the idea that the effects of globalization are mainly to be found in the area of hybridization, or creolization, which lead to an intercultural synthesis.

Evidence for all these contradictory effects of globalization can be found in the built environment. But although it is possible, for example, to point to the multicultural, multiform nature of urban regions around the world as a sign of growing heterogeneity, the strongest arguments seem to favour the homogenization viewpoint. The worldwide presence of chain stores and fast food restaurants and of advertisements for universally available consumer goods, from Sony to Marlboro to Nike, are the most obvious manifestations of homogenization. But there are plenty of other indications. One is the fact that cities and agglomerations around the world have undergone comparable developments and assumed similar shapes. Wherever one looks there seem to be high-rise downtowns, low-rise suburbs, urban peripheries with motorway cultures and business parks and so on. And everywhere the accompanying architecture has assumed a certain expressionlessness. Nowhere is this trend clearer than in the Asian metropolises, in recent years the subject of numerous reports in professional publications which describe, with a mixture of astonishment and admiration, the feverish development activities in cities like Seoul and Shanghai.

All around the world - or at least in the northern hemisphere - the sea of nondescript structures is dotted with the products of members of the architectural jet set, a good deal of whose work is nowadays carried out beyond their national borders. It is a greatly expanded jet set, incidentally. The foreign architects with commissions in the Netherlands alone already number in the dozens, from Philip Johnson to Diener & Diener and from Fumihico Maki to Charles Vandenhove. Their buildings stand as beacons in a

Michael Graves, Portland Building, Portland, USA, 1980

sea of uniformity, yet their very singularity gives them an oddly misplaced quality - especially when they are deliberately offered as an alternative to the surrounding meaninglessness, as Rem Koolhaas noted in 'Globalization' in *S,M,L,XL* (New York/Rotterdam, 1995) with reference to the work of Michael Graves: 'Beyond Florida, there is an entire "Michael Graves World" in Japan - more than 40 projects, from skyscrapers to city halls for small villages, mimetic devices for a culture unfamiliar with the initial sources, belated signs of a public domain they never had, and never will have. *Rome imported via New Jersey to Japan*, the literal collapse of time and place.'

To speak of a collapse of time and place in relation to the work of Graves is a sign perhaps of a somewhat over-developed sense of drama, but stripped of the overstatement there remains an idea that is now generally accepted, namely that it seems as if everything can happen everywhere nowadays, if need be simultaneously. This phenomenon whereby scarcely anything is tied to a particular place any more has long been an economic axiom but is now being seen as a fait accompli in architecture as well. The same building, with a few site-specific adjustments, can stand anywhere. It would be interesting to know to what extent the recent emergence of the idea that everything can stand everywhere is connected with the development of this architectural jet set who observe with their own eyes that the same things are to be found everywhere and now know from their own international practice that the same building can be built anywhere.

AUTHENTICITY

The realization that theoretically everything can stand everywhere, undermines the postmodern dogma that architecture must always have a unique, authentic relationship with the context. That dogma was already divorced from reality, for in retrospect a lot of postmodernist architecture is not much different from the *Ersatz* architecture which came in for such a drubbing in Charles Jencks's *The Language of Post-Modern Architecture* (London, 1977). What postmodern architecture had to offer was in many cases not much more than a (sometimes) historicizing decor, whether it was Quinlan Terry's office complex in Richmond, Charles Moore's Piazza d'Italia in New Orleans, Ricardo Bofill's famous complexes in the *villes nouvelles* of Paris (Marne-la-Vallée and St. Quentin-en-Yvelines) or some postmodernist ensemble or other with columns and porticoes: all these projects are deliberately intended as representations of authenticity, identity and meaning, the same qualities that crowds of tourists are increasingly searching for in vain these days. A similar artificial identity, intended to suggest the security of 'small town America', can be found in Seaside and that other triumph of New Urbanism in the United States, Celebration. This garden city for 20,000 inhabitants in

Charles Moore, Piazza d'Italia, New Orleans, USA, 1975-1978

Florida is being developed by the Disney Corporation which has abandoned its core business of amusement for the occasion and turned project developer. This is nothing short of sensational for a company that rose to prominence on the back of cartoon shorts and animated films, but oddly enough this pioneering switch has produced little reaction, despite the fact that it contains sufficient grounds for yet another outburst of cultural pessimism about the Disney-fication of the world.

Celebration is a reanimation of the ideal American suburb in a form that has never existed anywhere,

The Jerde Partnership, Universal CityWalk, Los Angeles, USA, 1990-1993

except perhaps in films about the golden 1950s and 60s, but which strikes everybody as familiar. This edited version containing the finest qualities of the American suburb belongs to the same category as the antiseptic CityWalk, the Universal Studios theme park in which all the highlights of Los Angeles are clustered together on one site. Rumour has it that this artificial LA is more popular with the local population than the run-down original.

The same method of compression is deployed in one of the latest showpieces of Las Vegas, the New York New York hotel-casino, in which the Empire State Building, the Chrysler Building and a handful of other famous New York structures have been recreated at one-third their real size and placed side by side. The compression method has been employed elsewhere in the casino capital on Las Vegas itself: in the roofing-over of the oldest part of the city, Fremont Street, designed, like CityWalk, by The Jerde Partnership. The roofing job has turned Fremont Street into a succession of individual casinos within a single spatial unity. The brightly lit facades form much the same sort of decor as the baroque Roman architecture in the shopping mall tacked on to Caesar's Palace. The only difference between the roofed-over Fremont Street and all those hotel-casinos that take their theme from the future (Stardust), the past (Luxor, Excalibur), exotic places or literature (Treasure Island), is that the theme of the refurbished Fremont Street is Las Vegas itself.

The themed casinos of Las Vegas, a theme park like CityWalk or a garden city like Celebration inevitably raise the question of what is or is not considered misplaced in architecture nowadays. On the one hand, given their universally accessible symbolism, they satisfy the postmodern requirement of intelligibility. On the other hand, they sin against another moralistic dogma of postmodernism, namely sensitivity to context. Within their own boundaries, Celebration, the Las Vegas casinos and CityWalk all possess coherence, an inner logic, but externally they form autonomous enclaves in a built context with which they actually have nothing to do. CityWalk is in Los Angeles, of which it is an echo, but it might just as well have been located a hundred or a thousand

Gaskin & Bezanski, New York, New York Hotel & Casino, Las Vegas, USA, 1995-1997

The Jerde Partnership, Canal City Hakata, Fukuoka, Japan, 1996

The Jerde Partnership, Fremont Street Experience, Las Vegas, USA, 1995

kilometres away. The covered-in Fremont Street could just as well have been a themed hotel in Reno, Atlantic City or any other gambling city in the United States, and a second Celebration could be built in any suburban environment in the United States. This autonomy applies to much contemporary architecture and urbanism, and not just in the United States. Enclaves are springing up all over the place, turning cities and urbanized regions into a succession of autonomous worlds that have little or nothing to do with their surroundings.

AIRPORT

Nowhere is the process of enclave formation stronger than in the field of airport architecture. All over the world, the major airports have grown into complex and multifaceted mega-structures that not only offer space for more terminals, piers and hangars than ever before, but also accommodate a growing number of functions that have nothing whatever to do with aviation. In many cases, these other functions make a bigger contribution to airport turnover than activities directly connected with air travel.

Airports are to the 1990s what museums were to the postmodern 1980s: the arena where numerous contemporary themes converge and all kinds of interesting developments take place and as such a natural focus of attention. The museum, the depository of significant objects, was a building type made to measure for the values espoused by postmodernism. It was also the source of a host of architectural innovations, thanks to the boom in commissions in this field. It began with Hans Hollein's Museum am Abteiberg in Mönchengladbach, one of the first museums where the building and the manner of presentation received as much attention as the collection. This was followed by the construction, renovation and expansion of a whole host of museums, especially in Germany: from Stirling's Neue Staatsgalerie in Stuttgart and the impressive Museumufer in Frankfurt am Main, to OMA's unrealized showpiece, the Kunst- und Medienzentrum in Karlsruhe, and Daniel Libeskind's Jewish Museum in Berlin. But even outside Germany there were plenty of new museums built, of which Josef Kleihues's ICA in Chicago and Frank Gehry's Guggenheim Museum in Bilbao are only two of the most recent examples. As well as attracting architectural interest, the museum has also been the focus of sociological interest in recent years because of the way it has started to function as semi-public space and as a tourist destination.

For similar reasons it is now the airport that is the focus of interest. Mobility, accessibility and infra-

Hans Hollein, Städtisches Museum am Abteiberg, Mönchengladbach, Germany, 1983

structure are seen as fundamental themes of the age, unlimited access to the world as the ideal of the moment. Moreover, air traffic has experienced worldwide exponential growth which has in turn sparked off another worldwide chain reaction of new or expanded facilities for air travel. This has given rise in recent years to an unmistakable architectural airport aesthetic, the main ingredients of which are an exposed steel construction (a space-frame or gigantic trusses), a marked preference for vaulted roofs, a colour palette of grey, white, pale blue and light green and, above all, acres and acres of glass.

The implications of airport development stretch a good deal further than the architecture alone. The growth of airports, and especially their expansion to embrace all sorts of functions not directly connected with air transport, has unavoidable planning consequences because of the increasing claim on space. What is more, thanks to all the offices, banks, hotels, restaurants, conference facilities, casinos and shopping centres in the immediate vicinity, the airport has developed into an significant economic centre that is sometimes so large that the airport starts to compete with the very city it was originally intended to serve. And, finally, the terminal building, tax-free shopping centres and transit lounges have been discovered as a fertile area for sociological research into an intriguing form of human behaviour: killing time while waiting for the next flight. The enclosed world of the terminal building is inhabited twenty-four hours a day by huge numbers of people, often from all corners of the world, who are there more or less of their own free will but who must at the same time submit to an enforced stay until their plane leaves in the company of fellow-travellers with whom they have absolutely no connection. At least as interesting is the ease with which just about anybody is able to find their way around any airport even on their first visit.

. The airport is an attractive model for the kind of existence that is nowadays associated with globalization, a world where 'jet lag' is built into everybody's biological clock and time and place have become utterly relative. As Rem Koolhaas - himself no mean frequent flyer, witness the statistics at the beginning of *S,M,L,XL* indicating that he was good for 360,000 kilometres in 1993 - pointed out in *Generic City*: 'In terms of its iconography/performance, the airport is a concentrate of both the hyper-local and the hyper-global - hyper-global in the sense you can get goods there that are not available even in the city, hyper-local in the sense you can get things there that you get nowhere else.'

The notion that the modern airport encapsulates the essence of this age of globalization turns up in countless books and magazine articles: 'The terminal concourses are the ramblas and agoras of the future

Frank O. Gehry & Associates, Guggenheim Museum Bilbao, Bilbao, Spain, 1991-1997

city, time-free zones where all the clocks of the world are displayed, an atlas of arrivals and destinations forever updating itself, where we briefly become true world citizens.' Thus the novelist J.G. Ballard in an ode to his favourite building type, published in *Blueprint* in September 1997. According to him, true happiness resides in the airport: 'I've long suspected that people are only truly happy and aware of a real purpose to their lives when they hand over their tickets at the check-in.' Similar sentiments, though less poetically expressed, are to be found in 'Planes of existence', an article by Marc Spiegler in the July/August 1997 issue of *Metropolis*. In it he highlights the way O'Hare International Airport is drawing more and more business activity away from the centre of Chicago and developing into a 'new type of edge city'.

Spiegler is not the first to have observed that the city centre is losing its prominence. In the mid-1980s, for example, Willem Jan Neutelings published a manifesto about what he termed the 'ring culture' in the journal *Vlees & beton* (no. 10) in which he claimed that throughout Europe the zones around orbital motorways were rapidly developing into linear urban centres, the ideal site for concert halls, DIY centres, exhibition centres, motels, sports parks and camping grounds. According to Neutelings, these linear centres are starting to replace congested historical town centres. The ring roads in the periphery are surrounded by 'the last large open spaces in the urban agglomerations which, because of their central location between city centre and suburbs, are able to guarantee the degree of public accessibility demanded by these kinds of mass functions'.

That airports, infrastructural nodes and motorways should be the modern catalysts of urbanization is every bit as logical as the emergence in earlier times of human settlements at the spot where two roads intersected or a river was fordable. The essential difference is that this time round it is accompanied by the decline of the city centre as the hub of urban life (although this decline is not as rapid as is sometimes claimed), leading to a complete transformation of the concept of the classic city as a self-contained entity into just one element in an omnipresent urban territory. This observation can be found, for instance, in Paulo Desideri's *Città di latta; favelas di lusso, autogrill, svincoli stradali e antenne paraboliche* (Genoa, 1995), in which he describes the difference between the experience of the train traveller who is deposited right in the middle of the city and the motorist, whose acquaintance with the city begins on the periphery. Even outside the city limits the motorist is almost continuously in an urbanized corridor. Desideri offers the Rome-Pescara autostrada as an example of the tin city from the title of his book. It is significant that it is the A 25, which runs through one of the most extensive scenic areas of Italy, the Abruzzi, that strikes him as urbanized. The route bears no comparison with any metropolitan region whatsoever but it is nonetheless perceived as urbanized because there is scarcely any point along its length from which there are no buildings to be seen. This example is a reflection not only of the degree of urbanization in Europe but also of the sensitivity to the phenomenon.

According to Spiegler, the urbanized zones alongside motorways and around airports, with their shopping malls, cultural amenities, convention centres but above all warehouses, supply depots, storage sheds and parking lots will eventually undergo the same process as the city centres. O'Hare Airport will have to contend with the same problems that have led to the exodus from downtown Chicago, such as rising land prices and increasing inaccessibility. The most likely outcome is a 'nebulous sprawl, transforming Chicago into a sort of heartland Los Angeles.'

Since the early 1990s, Los Angeles has been a much-cited example of the future of the city in the Western world, an interminable urbanized area with no coherent form, no hierarchical structure, no centre and no unity: a heteropolis, in the words of Charles Jencks who has described the phenomenon in South California under this name (*Heteropolis: Los Angeles, the riots and the strange beauty of hetero-architecture* (London/Berlin, 1993)). The same phenomenon manifests itself in Asia where Tokyo, Singapore, Hongkong, Shanghai and dozens of other metropolises constitute the Eastern version of the heteropolis. There is no plan-in-outline for the heteropolis, it is a product

Renzo Piano, Kansai Air Terminal, Osaka Bay, Japan, 1988-1994

Renzo Piano, Kansai Air Terminal, Osaka Bay, Japan, 1988-1994

of a pragmatic *laissez-faire* approach devoid of artistic pretensions since 'Planning makes no difference', to quote one of the propositions in Koolhaas's *Generic City*.

It is typical of this age that the heteropolis should be described primarily in terms of negatives, as a city without form or plan, without structure or centre, where even the architecture seems to be characterized mainly by an absence of distinguishing marks, by neutrality.

NEUTRALITY

One area where the neutrality of contemporary architecture is most evident is in its relationship to the context. It seems that architecture is capable of being just as footloose as all those internationally operating corporations nowadays known as 'global players' rather than 'multinationals' because they no longer have specific ties with any one nation. In architecture these specific ties usually consist of references to the context and to the history of the building site. Since the early 1990s, more and more buildings have been built worldwide whose sole involvement with their context consists of toeing the building line. For this architecture the surroundings constitute neither legitimation nor inspiration for these are derived from what goes on inside the building, from the programme. This autonomy is in many cases reinforced by the fact that the building has an inscrutable exterior that betrays nothing of what happens inside.

In this respect, too, supermodern architecture is essentially different from the postmodern variety whose practitioners always tried to find some way of expressing the building's purpose, either by following the conventions of building typology or by adding symbolic pointers. In supermodern architecture this rarely if ever happens. In many instances these buildings look as if they might house just about anything: an office or a school, a bank or a research centre, a hotel or apartments, a shopping mall or an airport terminal.

Neutrality can be seen as a reaction to the postmodernist and deconstructivist tendency to design everything, from building to doorknob, from furniture to coffee pot. This Midas touch reached into the farthest corners of public space, for even the most peripheral residential areas bristle with offbeat rubbish bins, street lamps, benches, railings and the like that have 'creative design' written all over them. The result is that the world is chock-full of signs. In reaction there is now an alternative approach in which objects are sufficient in themselves and are not required to convey anything. Yet the neutrality of contemporary architecture is not merely a negation, for blankness has a positive side as well, even if it is more difficult to specify for the moment because the conceptual framework of architecture is still so strongly tied up with postmodern notions. Whereas postmodernist and deconstructivist architecture almost always contained a message, today architecture is increasingly conceived as an empty medium. Nowhere is that more evident than in the fashion for 'inscribed' buildings, structures whose smooth facades are covered with fixed or moving text and images. The text is an addition to an intrinsically expressionless form, just like the label on a can of soup.

The buildings to which such texts are applied are for the most part orthogonal boxes. For that matter, the neutral box, the modernist ideal anathematized by the postmodernists, is very much in vogue again for buildings without text, too. The neutrality of the rectangle is often emphasized by giving the facades a smooth finish, for example with glass, so that they evoke a sense of insubstantial superficiality. But even if the absence of substance is accentuated by the transparency, this does not mean that these buildings are completely anonymous. In many cases, considered use of materials and detailing gives this architecture an aesthetic refinement comparable to the work of the master of this technique, Ludwig Mies van der Rohe. Whereas the postmodernists regarded his superior simplicity as dull - wittily expressed in Venturi's distortion of Mies's famous dictum as 'less is a bore' - nowadays architects are rediscovering the richness of simplicity. One explanation for this might be that an architecture that refers to nothing outside itself and makes no appeal to the intellect, automatically prioritizes direct experience, the sensory experience of

Renzo Piano, Bercy 2 Shopping Centre, Paris, France, 1987-1990

Massimiliano Fuksas, SPAR Supermarket Europark, Salzburg, Austria, 1996

space, material and light. In an age when nobody is surprised by anything any more, it appears that ever stronger stimuli are required to arouse the senses. This pursuit of extreme sensations manifests itself not only in the super-cool transparency and smoothness of glazed buildings, but equally in the tactile massiveness of the sculptural volumes that have been appearing in recent years. However different in outward appearance, the monolithic sculptures are the

Bernard Tschumi, Glass Video Pavilion, Groningen, the Netherlands, 1990

other side of the coin from the transparent boxes: architecture based on a radical reduction that is used to conjure up an exceptionally strong impression.

The impression made by this architecture is created not at the level of messages to be articulated, but at the emotional level, by the atmosphere. The even, smooth and flowing spaces of OMA's Educatorium at Utrecht University are every bit as typical of this approach as the strongly contrasted massivity of another building on the same campus, Neutelings Riedijk's Minnaert Building.

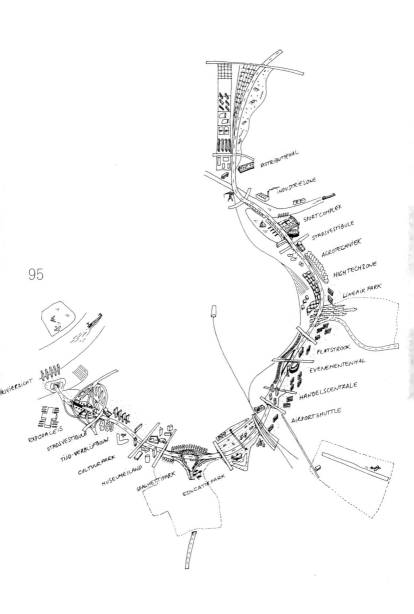

Willem Jan Neutelings, development model for 'Ring van Antwerpen', Belgium, 1986

In both the Educatorium and the Minnaert Building, construction and technology play an important role. The structural ingenuity of the Educatorium is most evident in the folded concrete plate that transmutes seamlessly from floor to roof. In the Minnaert Building the most striking example of technical ingenuity is the way natural ventilation and rainwater are used for cooling. The interest in construction technology and building physics displayed in these two buildings is

Dominique Perrault, Hôtel Industriel Berlier, Paris, France, 1985-1990

indicative of the recent furore surrounding the technological aspect of architecture, which had all but disappeared during the postmodernist ascendancy. During the 1970s and 80s the only architects actively engaged in exploring the limits of construction and technology were those designated as 'high tech'. Whereas in those days designers like Norman Foster, Richard Rogers and Renzo Piano were outsiders in an architectural world geared to symbolic representation, in the 1990s their approach has gained in prestige. Indeed, the notion that architects should try to apply the latest insights in the field of construction, technology and materials, once regarded as idiosyncratic, seems to be fully accepted nowadays. The change of heart began under deconstructivism whose proponents, primarily for aesthetic reasons, were keen to build impossible-looking architecture. Since then, the pursuit of unparalleled structural feats has really taken off, although the most spectacular examples have not - or at least not yet - been realized. This is true of OMA's design of an enormous

transparent plastic dome for a Sea Terminal in Zeebrugge and of Jean Nouvel's plan to erect a *Tour sans Fins* in the Parisian business district of La Défense: a 420-metre skyscraper with a transparent top by virtue of which the building seems to dissolve rather than end. One of the intriguing structural aspects of this tower is the huge pendulum that will be suspended inside, its great weight hanging in a tank of silicon oil, in order to absorb the wind forces exerted on the top of the building.

Transparency, incidentally, is a major theme of Nouvel's work, as witness his Fondation Cartier in

Paris, a building whose facades consist almost entirely of glass. Not least because of the glass screen placed in front of it, the Fondation Cartier scarcely seems to be a building at all. And this makes it a completely different kind of structure from something like Bernard Tschumi's transparent video pavilion in Groningen, built in the context of the *What a wonderful world* festival. In this lopsided orthogonal box, form predominates over transparency. Where this pavilion is first and foremost an object, the Fondation Cartier seems like a assemblage of transparent slabs between

Dominique Perrault, Bibliothèque Nationale de France, Paris, France, 1989-1996

which, on closer inspection, lurks a building. Nouvel has used glass in a quite different way in Galeries Lafayette in Berlin where it is the material's smoothness rather than its transparency that predominates.

These two properties of glass, on the one hand transparency or translucency, and on the other hand extreme smoothness, are nowadays, thanks to technological advances in the use of self-supporting

Iñaki Abelos & Juan Herreros, Municipal Gymnasium, Simancas, Spain, 1989-1992

glass, the development of better adhesives and so on, being deployed in a superior form, not only by Nouvel but by numerous architects, from Dominique Perrault (*hôtel industriel* Berlier, Bibliothèque Nationale, both in southeastern Paris) to Iñaki Abalos & Juan Herreros (building for the Ministry of the Interior in Madrid).

As such, we are closer than ever before to achieving the modernist ideal of a totally transparent architecture. The desire for total transparency manifested itself in the 1920s in Mies van der Rohe's unrealized designs for a skyscraper in Berlin's Friedrichstrasse and in the late 1940s in Philip Johnson's Glass House, but only now does technology seem to be sufficiently sophisticated to make that much-prized total transparency a reality. In a way, contemporary architecture is thus a superlative version of the modern architecture of the interwar years and the first decade after the Second World War.

102

* For an overview of various sociological viewpoints see:

- Mike Featherstone, Scott Lash, Roland Robertson (eds) *Global Modernities* (London, 1995)
- Ulf Hannerz, *Transnational Connections* (London/New York, 1996)
- David Clark, *Urban World/Global City* (London/New York, 1996)
- John Eade (ed.), *Living the Global City: Globalization as a local process* (London/New York, 1997)
- Alan Scott (ed.), *The Limits of Globalization: Cases and Arguments* (London/New York, 1997)
- Paul Smith, *Millennial Dreams: Contemporary Culture and Capital in the North* (London/New York, 1997)

Iñaki Abelos & Juan Herreros, Building for the Ministry of the Interior, Madrid, Spain, 1991-1993

Herzog & De Meuron, Ricola Europe Factory and Storage Building, Mulhouse-Brunnstatt,

France, 1992-1993

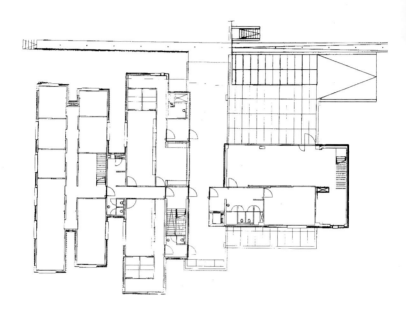

Wiel Arets, Police station, Boxtel, the Netherlands, 1994-1997

108

Jean Nouvel, Cartier Foundation for Contemporary Art and

Head Office of Cartier France, Paris, France, 1991-1994

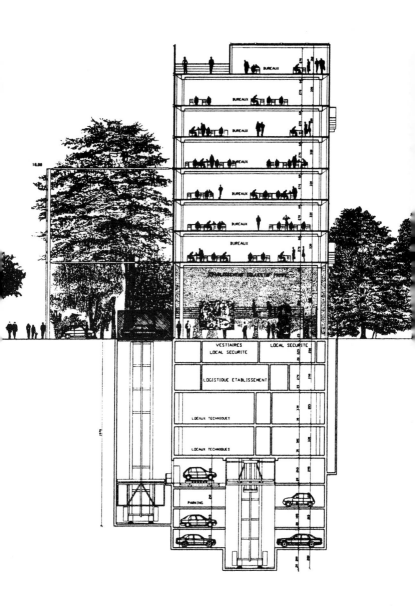

Jean Nouvel, Cartier Foundation for Contemporary Art and Head Office of Cartier
France, Paris, France, 1991-1994

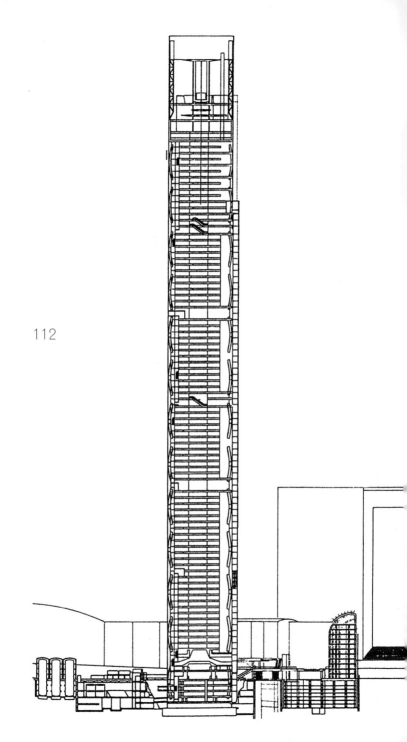

112

Jean Nouvel, Tour sans Fins (prize-winning project), La Défense - Paris, France, 1989

Jean Nouvel, Cartier-Interdica Factory, Fribourg, Switzerland, 1989-1990

Jean Nouvel, Galeries Lafayette, Berlin, Germany, 1991-1996

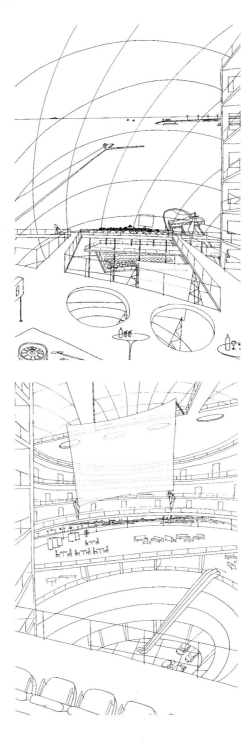

OMA, Sea Terminal, Zeebrugge, Belgium, 1989

120

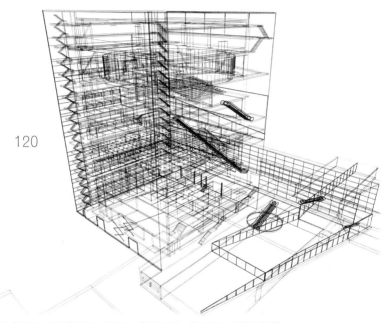

OMA, Kunst- und Medienzentrum, Karlsruhe, Germany, 1989-1992

OMA, Educatorium, Utrecht, the Netherlands, 1997

125

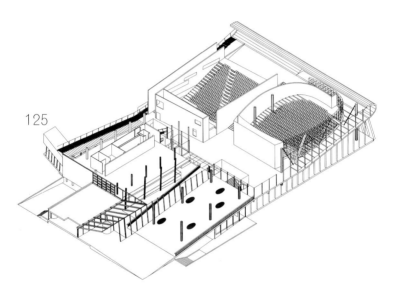

OMA, Educatorium, Utrecht, the Netherlands, 1997

Arata Isozaki, Okayama West Police Station, Okayama, Japan, 1993-1996

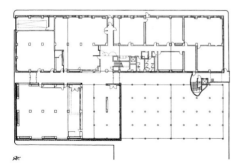

A Superr
Perspect

128

odern

ve

The 1990s have seen the emergence of a fully fledged replacement for postmodernism, deconstructivism and all the mini-movements that have followed in their wake. This successor did not suddenly appear from one day to the next but has steadily taken shape over the space of several years. One of the clearest signs of this gradual change of course with respect to postmodernism is the changed attitude towards modernism. The almost contemptuous aversion to modernism displayed by postmodernist and deconstructivist architects has given way to a more nuanced view. And although this has not resulted in a genuine revaluation of the architecture that dominated the Western world in the 1950s and 60s, it has led to new interest in the modernist aesthetic and to a revival of the idea that the processes of modernization are the driving force behind architectural and urbanist innovation.

Another essential difference between the architecture of a decade ago and of the present day, is the attitude towards symbolism. Symbolism was fundamental to both postmodernism and deconstructivism, whereby postmodernist architecture was usually a vehicle for symbolic messages and deconstructivist architecture a metaphor for non-architectural concepts. Recent architecture reflects a declining interest in accommodating a symbolic cargo or rendering a - sometimes only half-understood - philosophical or scientific idea.

The waning interest in this symbolic dimension is evident, for example, in the search for the absolute zero of architecture such as that undertaken by the entrants in a competition for a House with No Style (1992) organized by the journal *Japan Architect* and devised and judged by Rem Koolhaas. Unlike the recent designs for a virtual house published in *Any*

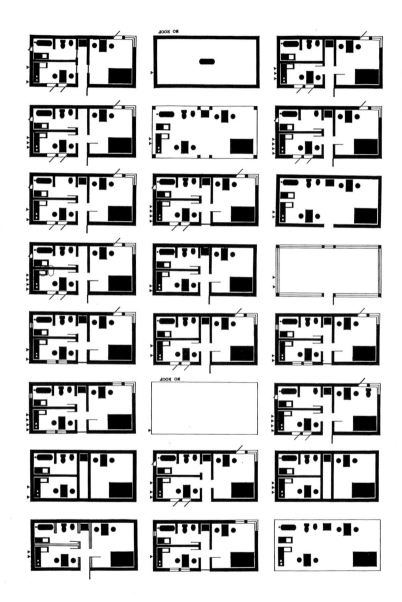

Yusoke Fujiki, prize-winning design for the House with No Style competition, 1992

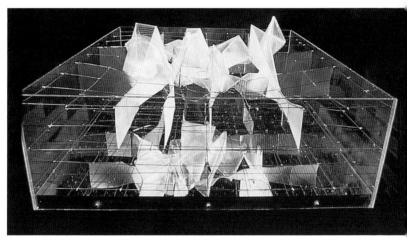

Peter Eisenman, The Virtual House, 1997

magazine, which can be interpreted as just one more attempt to find an architectural metaphor for a topical theme - in this case cyberspace - the *JA*'s competition was intended to arrive at an architecture devoid of allusion.

To say that architects are searching for an architecture without symbolic or metaphorical allusions is not to imply that there is no meaning at all any more. Just that the tendency of postmodernists and deconstructivists to look for hidden meanings everywhere has become largely superfluous for the simple reason that, more often than not, there is no hidden meaning. In its place we now have a form of meaning that is derived directly from how the architecture looks, how it is used and, above all, how it is experienced. After postmodernist and deconstructivist architecture, which appealed primarily to the intellect, a new architecture is evolving which attaches greater importance to visual, spatial and tactile sensation.

The disappearance of the compulsive tendency to construe everything in symbolic terms, has not only freed the designer from an onerous duty to keep on producing 'meaningful' architecture, but has also made it possible for architects, critics and historians to view architecture differently in that things are now accepted phenomenologically for what they are. The moralism and dogmatism implicit in postmodernism have made way for realism. Such realism is to be found, for example, in Dominique Perrault's *hôtel industriel*, an alien and totally self-sufficient glass box in the disorderly context of the Parisian *boulevard périphérique*. As Perrault described it in 1990: 'Nothing, less than nothing, no anchorage, no hold, no hook. no soothing theories about the city with-parks-and-gardens but a confrontation with "our world", that one, the true, the so-called "hard" world, the world people claim not to want.'

The laconic acceptance of things as they are, is also indicative of a real change in the fundamental intellectual stance of both architect and critic. The echo of the avant-garde attitude of disapproval and resistance that was audible in postmodernism and deconstructivism, has completely died away. In that respect contemporary architecture bears an unmistakable resemblance to the least critical phase of modernism, during the 1950s and 60s, when there was a strong tendency to accept prevailing conditions as inescapable facts. Now, as then, architecture is (fairly straightforwardly) at the service of modernization which is currently most visible in the processes of globalization.

The phenomenological approach gives rise to a different retrospective view of architecture previously interpreted mainly as symbolic representation or as the articulation of ideas. From a postmodern perspective, for example, the most important feature of Jean Nouvel's Institut du Monde Arabe in Paris was the facade with diaphragm windows because this was seen as a high-tech reference to the screens used in traditional Arab architecture. The other, unarticulated facade, was in postmodernist terms a leftover, its sole, minimal form of contextualism, a silk-screen print on glass of the silhouette of the historical buildings visible from the IMA. From a supermodern viewpoint, however, this is the more interesting facade precisely because of its total independence from the context and the absence of any hint of accommodation. Another building open to a fresh, non-postmodernist interpretation is OMA's Kunsthal in Rotterdam. Rather than being seen as an ingenious fusion of Mies van der Rohe's Nationalgalerie, Le Corbusier's Musée de Croissance Illimitée and a multi-storey car park or as a reflection of Koolhaas's ideas about the city, urbanity and architecture, the Kunsthal is interesting because of the intriguing variety of spatial experiences it provides.

The same change of perspective also influences the perception of the built environment as a whole. In the past few years there have been a great many articles, books and special magazine issues devoted to what would until recently have been seen as formless and meaningless: the urban periphery, the motorway, the unplanned, the informal and the commercial architecture of shopping malls and business parks. In all these publications the authors are searching for an inner logic and for points of reference that might enable them to understand something that initially appears to be meaningless. Mirko Zardini, for example, in his contribution to *Paesaggi ibridi: un viaggio nella città contemporanea* (Hybrid landscapes: a journey through the contemporary city; Milan, 1996), proposes breathing new life into the notion of 'picturesqueness'. It would, he claims, make it possible to arrive at a positive assessment of characteristics that until now have been viewed negatively, such as heterogeneity, excessive change, disorder and incongruity. The abstraction of Zardini's proposal is typical of all explorative efforts so far, including the present one, to assign meaning to what has long been regarded as a meaningless mass. But this is a natural phase in the development of every new frame of reference, for it is always necessary to first shake off the previous concepts. Given the overwhelming number of designs, buildings and publications pointing in the direction of a new conception of architecture and the built environment, one can safely predict that it is only a question of time before these give rise to a new frame of reference with sufficient subtlety to act as a self-affirming system, just as happened twenty years ago with postmodernism's approach geared to symbolic representation.

The new frame of reference - unlike that of postmodernism and deconstructivism - will no longer be dictated by the unique, the authentic or the specific, but by the universal. These days both architects and critics are endeavouring to develop a genuine rapport with the everyday environment, including in its most arbitrary, monotonous and ugly forms. In the age of globalization, with banality manifesting itself on an overwhelming scale, such efforts are more necessary than ever.

OMA, Kunsthal, Rotterdam, the Netherlands, 1988-1992

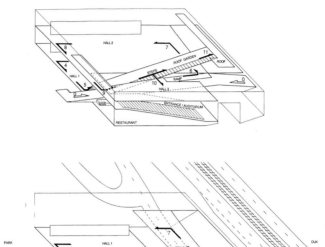

OMA, Kunsthal, Rotterdam, the Netherlands, 1988-1992

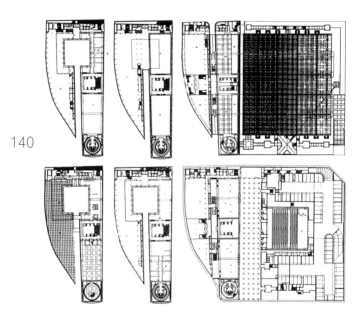

Jean Nouvel, Institut du Monde Arabe, Paris, France, 1981-1987

Jean Nouvel, Institut du Monde Arabe, Paris, France, 1981-1987

Illustration Credits

Colophon

This publication was in part made possible by a grant from The Netherlands Architecture Fund.

Design: Joseph Plateau, Amsterdam
Translation: Robyn de Jong-Dalziel
Picture Editors: Patricia Molegraaf, Ingrid Oosterheerd
Printing: Drukkerij Waanders, Zwolle
Production: Marianne Lahr
Publisher: Simon Franke

Available in North, South and Central America through D.A.P./Distributed Art Publishers Inc, 155 Sixth Avenue 2nd Floor, New York, NY 10013-1507, Tel. 212 627.1999 Fax 212 627.9484

ISBN 90-5662-074-6